ANIMAL TESTING:
Lifesaving Research
VS.
Animal Welfare

by Lois Sepahban

Content Consultant
Seth M. Walker, M.A.
Department of Philosophy
University of Central Florida

COMPASS POINT BOOKS
a capstone imprint

ABOUT THE AUTHOR

Lois Sepahban has written several books for children, in areas such as science, history, biography, and fiction. She lives in Kentucky with her husband and two children.

SOURCE NOTES

Lifesaving Research

Page 10, line 23: "Federal Register Notice: New Drug and Biological Drug Products; Evidence Needed to Demonstrate Effectiveness of New Drugs When Human Efficacy Studies Are Not Ethical or Feasible; Final Rule." 31 May 2002. 26 April 2014. U.S. Food and Drug Administration. http://www.fda.gov/BiologicsBloodVaccines/DevelopmentApprovalProcess/InvestigationalNewDrugINDorDeviceExemptionIDEProcess/default.htm

Page 11, line 10: Susan Offner. "The Importance of Dissection in Biology Teaching." 3 March 1993. 4 June 2014. University of California Press. http://www.jstor.org/discover/10.2307/4449611?uid=3739680&uid=2133&uid=2&uid=70&uid=4&uid=3739256&sid=21103825966641

TABLE OF CONTENTS

Shared Resources

Chapter 1

A MORAL QUESTION

For three months undercover investigators with the Humane Society of the United States took video footage at Georgia Regents University's animal research lab in Augusta, Georgia. While there they met Shy Guy, a mixed-breed dog who had been sold to GRU by an animal dealer. Shy Guy and other dogs in GRU's lab were being used in dental implant experiments. Dental implants are fake teeth that replace missing teeth. Researchers pulled out the dogs' teeth and replaced them with implants. Researchers wanted to see how the dental implants they designed compared with dental implants designed by other companies. Eight weeks later, after testing was complete, Shy Guy and five other dogs were euthanized.

Dogs are often used in animal testing. One lab in the United Kingdom forced beagles to inhale cigarette smoke to test new cigarettes in 1975.

Dentists who reviewed the 2013 investigation came to two conclusions. First, the testing that was done on Shy Guy and the other dogs was for products that had already been approved by the Food and Drug Administration (FDA). This meant that the tests did not have to be repeated. Second, the same tests could have been done on human subjects who were already missing teeth.

The U.S. Department of Agriculture (USDA) inspected the research facility at GRU in December 2013. They found the lab had violated the Animal Welfare Act for many of the animals in its care. The act requires researchers to use nonanimal experiments whenever possible. The USDA was concerned that the dogs were not necessary in the dental experiments, so using them was a violation of the Animal Welfare Act.

A Widespread Problem

Georgia Regents University is not the only university in the United States that has been cited for violating the Animal Welfare Act. USDA inspectors found violations of the Animal Welfare Act at Harvard University. The violations included the deaths of two primates that became dehydrated because they were not given water. Their dehydration was so severe that they had to be euthanized. The USDA fined Harvard University $24,000 for 11 violations in 2011 and 2012.

USDA inspectors also found violations of the Animal Welfare Act at the University of Wisconsin–Madison. The violations included the deaths of a gerbil and a monkey that were not properly cared for. The USDA fined the university $35,000 for violations that occurred from 2007 to 2013.

The University of Pennsylvania keeps approximately 5,000 animals for research each year, more than any other Ivy League university. This number does not account for mice, rats, and birds, whose numbers do not have to be

The USDA allows for animal testing but requires that labs provide food, water, and shelter, even if the shelter is a small cage.

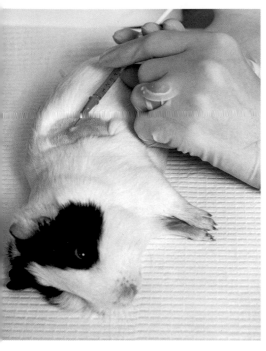

Guinea pigs are monitored under the Animal Welfare Act.

reported. Experts believe the total number of animals tested at the University of Pennsylvania to be much higher. The university was charged with violating the Animal Welfare Act in 2011. In one case a puppy slipped under a grate. By the time workers found it, the puppy had died. In another case three gerbils died from dehydration. Their water had been placed out of their reach.

Animal activists believe these violations of the Animal Welfare Act are cause for concern. The USDA requires research labs to provide safe shelter, food, and water for all animals. When labs do not provide water for gerbils or primates, when they do not keep careful watch over newborn puppies, and when they do not provide safe cages for monkeys, they are breaking the law. And when they kill dogs for dental experiments that never needed to be done, they are breaking trust with animals and with the public.

In his book *Dominion: The Power of Man, the Suffering of Animals, and the Call to Mercy*, author Matthew Scully said that animal testing is an act of cruelty that can lead to human cruelty. He argues that out of anyone, scientists should know that animal cruelty could lead to human cruelty toward other humans. But, he says, when animal testing scientists abandon their morals in the cruel treatment of animals, that cruelty can become a bad habit.

New Technology to Replace Animals

Roughly 25 million animals live in U.S. research labs today. But that number could soon be reduced. New technology, such as computer models and cloned tissue samples, is available to replace animals in experiments. There are also proposed laws that could make some kinds of animal testing illegal. These changes are already happening on a small scale. But for them to happen in all labs, society must first decide whether animal testing is wrong.

Chapter 2

PEOPLE ARE NOT MICE

People have been experimenting on animals for at least 2,000 years. Throughout history scientists have studied dead bodies to see how the human body is made. But in order to see how the body functions, scientists have to look at living bodies. At various times and in various places, scientists have used living humans as subjects for their experiments. It happened during World War II (1939–1945) when Nazi scientists experimented on unwilling prisoners in concentration camps. But most societies have condemned experiments on humans.

Unwilling to experiment on people, scientists turned to animals. In the 1600s scientists tested substances

A bird is deprived of air while onlookers observe the bird's reaction in Joseph Wright's 1760s painting.

on living animals to see how their bodies would react. This kind of testing is similar to what happens to lab animals today. The animal is used as a model for a human. Four hundred years ago, there was very little argument against animal experiments for two reasons. First, most people did not know about the experiments. And second, most people believed that animals didn't think and feel. This idea started to change in the 1700s and 1800s when scientists performed their experiments in public as entertainment.

After witnessing animals suffer during experiments, people began to argue against animal experimentation, calling it pointless and cruel. This began the antivivisection movement of the 1800s. Many famous people, including politicians, writers, and even Queen Victoria of Great Britain, supported the movement. Antivivisectionists believed experimenting on living animals was wrong. Animals might not be as intelligent as humans, they argued, but they were still able to suffer and feel.

Continued Use of Animals

In animal testing today, researchers experiment on living animals. They test new drugs and medicines on them. They test cosmetic products, such as makeup and perfume. They even injure animals to see how they will behave. At the end of the experiments, most animals are euthanized so scientists can study their body tissues and organs. Those who oppose animal testing think it should never be done, but it continues to happen with many more animals.

In animal experiments in the United States, approximately 95 percent of the animals are mice, rats, and birds. These animals are not protected by the Animal Welfare Act, so there is not an official count of them. A 2012 USDA report shows that 1.1 million animals that were covered by the Animal Welfare Act were used in labs. Based on that number, scientists estimate that anywhere from 13 million to 25 million mice and rats are used in research in the United States each year. Scientists deem rats and mice necessary for their research. They are experimented on and eventually killed.

The Animal Welfare Act does monitor the care of other research animals, including dogs, cats, chimpanzees, monkeys, rabbits, guinea pigs, and livestock, such as pigs and sheep. More than 72,000 dogs and 24,000 cats were used in research labs in the United States in 2012, the most recent year for which figures are available. Scientists use dogs and cats in organ transplant experiments and in experiments to learn more about cancer, diabetes, and

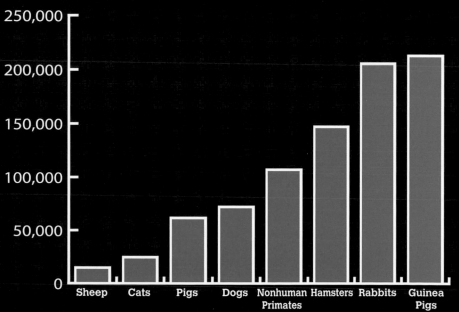

Number of Monitored Animal Welfare Act Animals Used in Labs in 2012

Some animals in animal shelters are sold to labs for testing.

allergies. One way labs get these cats and dogs is through pound seizures. Lab researchers purchase stray, lost, or abandoned cats and dogs from animal shelters. Pound seizure is legal in many states, and in Oklahoma, the law even requires animal shelters to sell dogs and cats to labs that request them. Another way labs get cats and dogs is through Class B animal dealers. The animal dealers get dogs and cats from individuals who give them away for free and from animal shelters. Then they sell the cats and dogs to research labs.

Chimpanzees, the animals most similar to humans, are also used in animal experiments. Roughly 1,000 chimpanzees live in research facilities in the United States. Because they are genetically similar to humans, chimpanzees have been used in experiments studying hepatitis, HIV, infectious diseases, and cancer. Despite this similarity, the Institute of Medicine, which is affiliated with the National Academy of Sciences, said the use of chimpanzees in research is not necessary. The IOM is an organization outside of the government that works to offer unbiased advice to policy makers and the public. Its 2011 report said alternatives to chimpanzee experiments should be used.

After the release of the 2011 IOM report the National Institutes of Health (NIH) temporarily banned the use of chimpanzees in biomedical testing. Chimpanzees are still used in behavioral testing. Several countries, including New Zealand and Japan, as well as the European Union, have strictly limited or even banned research using nonhuman great apes—chimpanzees, bonobos, gorillas, orangutans, and gibbons.

Nonhuman primates, including macaques, monkeys, and baboons, are also used in research. More than 100,000 primates were used in research labs in the United States in 2012. Scientists use primates to test new vaccines and drugs and to conduct experiments on obesity. They also study behavior in primates to learn more about humans.

Because rabbits are not aggressive, they are easy for scientists to handle, making them a common choice for animal testing experiments.

Rabbits are commonly used in research experiments because they are not aggressive. They are also inexpensive to buy and reproduce quickly, offering more test subjects. They are often used in experiments for cosmetics and household products and in studies to see if products harm a pregnant subject's fetus. More than 200,000 guinea pigs and hamsters were used in animal experiments in 2012. Hamsters and guinea pigs are often used in tests of drug safety and in experiments on pain without the use of pain relievers. Farm animals, such as pigs and sheep, are also used in animal experiments. In 2012, more than 61,000 pigs and 14,000 sheep were used in tests on organ transplants and reproductive systems.

A Rabbit Is a Rabbit

Scientists argue that the similarities between humans and nonhuman mammals are the reason animal experiments are successful. They point out that humans and rats, for example, share more than 95 percent of their DNA. But does that make rats close enough to humans for experiments to really work? Research scientists explained in the *National Academy of Sciences* journal that rats used in labs are obese and don't get enough exercise. They are so unhealthy that they are at a higher risk for getting cancer or other diseases. Living conditions for lab rats are far different from human living conditions. So when these unhealthy lab rats are used in experiments, the scientists said, the results can be misleading for humans.

Chimpanzees are even more closely related to humans than rats. But even though they share more than 98 percent of the same DNA, their bodies do not react the same way to disease. After 11 years of HIV research on chimpanzees, scientists from the NIH told Congress in 2000 that their research had little success. Chimpanzees infected with HIV never developed AIDS. The experience of chimpanzees with HIV is very different from the experience of humans with HIV. Most humans with HIV develop AIDS unless they take special drugs to keep HIV from growing. In spite of genetic similarities between chimpanzees and humans, chimpanzees' bodies reacted differently to HIV than human bodies.

A More Humane World

Scientists argue that animals are close enough to humans for experiments to work. But if so, then perhaps they are close enough to humans for animal experiments to be unethical. People on either side of the debate about animal experiments must answer this question: Is it ethical to experiment on animals? Those who support animal testing say that it is, especially if the experiments lead to knowledge or medications that save human lives.

Those who oppose animal testing say that it is not ethical to experiment on animals for any reason. The antivivisectionists argue that a society that supports animal testing supports cruelty. In their opinion, a society that supports animal testing believes the result is more important than the path to that result. That means that a new drug for humans is more important than all of the animals experimented on.

Antivivisectionists believe that people should treat animals in a humane way. They believe people should treat animals with compassion and mercy, just as they would another human.

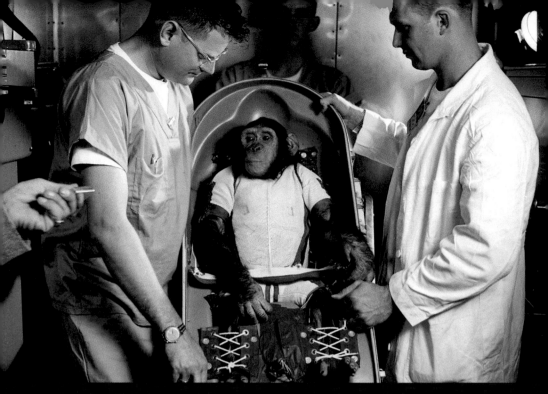

Ham the chimp became the first chimpanzee in space aboard the *Mercury-Redstone 2* in January 1961.

Chimpanzees in the Space Program

Beginning in 1959 the United States Air Force purchased 65 baby chimpanzees, most of which had been captured in the wild in Africa, for experiments in the space program. The baby chimps were used to see how space travel affected their bodies. Chimpanzees were used because of their genetic similarities to humans. Scientists preferred the baby chimps because they were smaller and easier to work with than adult chimps. The chimpanzees were sent into space for short trips and even to orbit Earth. On Earth chimpanzees were exposed to electric shock and acceleration. They were used in crash tests. The Air Force leased or sold most of their chimpanzees after the United States' first manned space flight in 1961. The chimpanzees were sent to zoos and research facilities. Today organizations such as Save the Chimps have set up facilities to provide safe homes for space program chimpanzees and their descendants.

Chapter 3

THE HUMAN COST OF ANIMAL TESTING

Animals are used in research experiments to benefit humans. In recent years, though, several experiments have gone wrong. In some cases experiments are safe for animals but dangerous for humans. Antivivisectionists argue that the only way to be certain that new medications are safe for people is to test them on people.

The NIH was hopeful about testing fialuridine on humans in 1993. If the testing went well, it would be used to treat hepatitis B. Fialuridine had passed safety tests on mice, rats, dogs, and monkeys. Fifteen people volunteered to test the drug. After taking fialuridine for 13 weeks, one of the volunteers had to be hospitalized

Brains of mice that were given AN-1792 did not show inflammation, leading researchers to believe it was safe for humans.

for liver failure. After that incident, all of the other volunteers stopped taking fialuridine. But six more volunteers went to the hospital with liver failure. Five of those volunteers died and the other two had to have liver transplants. Scientists think that the differences between nonhuman livers and human livers caused fialuridine to be safe for animals but not for humans.

Elan Corporation started testing AN-1792 on people as an Alzheimer's vaccine in 2000. But they stopped all human tests in January 2002. Four people tested had brain inflammation, which showed up as sores or injuries on the brain. The experimental vaccine caused inflammation in 18 volunteers. Researchers had earlier tested the vaccine on mice, but the mice did not show any of the same brain injuries.

Scientists working on the new drug TGN1412 were excited. It had passed animal safety tests on primates and was about to be tested on people to treat leukemia and rheumatoid arthritis. In the first human test, TGN1412 was given to six healthy people in 2006. They were given a dose that was 500 times less than the dose given to primates during safety tests. Within minutes, all six began to have bad reactions. The volunteers were rushed to the hospital because their organs were shutting down. TGN1412 worked in primates but not in humans, proving that in at least some cases, successful animal tests do not translate to successful or safe human products.

Draize Testing

The FDA does not require cosmetic products to be tested on animals. And many U.S. companies have phased it out because of new laws in Europe. China, however, requires cosmetics products to be tested on animals. U.S. cosmetics companies that want to market their products in China must still perform tests on animals. One test that is used infrequently today is called the Draize test. During the test an animal, usually a rabbit, is locked into a frame so it cannot move. Researchers then drip or rub products into the animal's eyes or skin. Researchers argue that they use the tests to see if the ingredients in their beauty products will be harmful to humans. But thousands of the ingredients have already been listed in an international database and categorized as safe. And the safety of new ingredients can be established using nonanimal tests. In addition, testing personal products on animals is not the best way to predict how safe they are for humans. Scientists can test products in vitro—on human cells in test tubes—sparing animals from the cruelty of painful tests.

Alternatives to Animal Tests

Research labs and scientists follow the 3Rs of animal testing : replace animals with new tests, reduce the number of animals used, and refine tests to cause less suffering. Today there are approximately 50 alternatives to animal tests. Scientists often test new vaccines and drugs on animals to test for contaminants. One way they do this is by injecting a substance into a rabbit to see what effect it has on the rabbit. As an alternative a company has developed a test to be used on blood donated by human volunteers.

There is also an alternative to Draize testing, which involves dripping or rubbing substances into an animal's eyes to observe its effects. Instead of testing hygiene products on animals, researchers test on skin tissue donated by people who need to have small amounts of skin removed during a surgery. New products are tested on the skin in a test tube.

Computer simulations are another alternative. They can be used to predict how a chemical will affect the human body. These tests can save animals from being used in toxicity tests, which show whether a chemical will be poisonous. In addition, products and ingredients listed as Generally Recognized as Safe (GRAS) have already been approved by the FDA. They do not need to be retested.

Chapter 4

A MORE HUMANE FUTURE

Many research facilities in the United States are given government funding for their projects. The NIH spent almost $15 billion on research that involved animal testing in 2014. And polls indicate most Americans support animal testing. But that support is changing. Ninety percent of Americans supported animal testing in 1949. That number had dropped to 57 percent by 2013. Antivivisectionists are using the shift in attitudes to focus on two areas of animal testing: ending all testing on great apes and ending cosmetics testing on animals.

Chimps enjoy a snack at Primarily Primates, one of the oldest ape sanctuaries in the United States, located in Texas.

The Great Ape Protection Act

The goal of the Great Ape Protection Act is to end invasive experiments, such as the use of vaccines, on all great apes. Proponents say it would save the U.S. government approximately $25 million. Instead of being tested in labs, great apes would be placed in sanctuaries, which is far less expensive than maintaining and caring for them in labs.

The Great Ape Protection Act has almost 200 sponsors in the House of Representatives and the Senate. It has been introduced in Congress every year since 2008.

But supporters of experimentation on chimpanzees block it every year, despite widespread support.

Animal protection groups, such as the Humane Society of the United States and the Physicians Committee for Responsible Medicine, have been working with members of Congress to get the Great Ape Protection Act passed. During the 112th Congress, from 2011 to 2013, the bill moved out of committee. As in previous years, it was blocked. But supporters of the bill are hopeful because it gains more support every year.

Banning Animal Tests of Cosmetics

Many personal care products people use every day— makeup, toothpaste, and shampoo—are tested on animals.

Chimps Deserve Better

Jody is a 35-year-old chimp. She has spent most of her life in research labs, where she gave birth to at least nine babies. Jody and all of her babies were experimented on. She was removed from a lab in Pennsylvania in 2008. Today she lives at a chimpanzee sanctuary.

Wild chimpanzees live in social groups, spending their time grooming each other, foraging for food, and building nests. Life for chimpanzees in research labs is quite different. Chimpanzees at research labs live in small metal cages. Approximately 1,000 chimpanzees still live in research labs where they are experimented on. The Humane Society of the United States started a campaign, called Chimps Deserve Better, to end animal testing on chimpanzees. Its goal is to retire all chimps living in research facilities to sanctuaries.

During animal testing, such as this 1959 Draize testing experiment in Syracuse, New York, rabbits are placed in restraints.

Testing of these products can include eye and skin irritation tests, such as the Draize test. They are often tested on animals even after all of their ingredients have been accepted as safe by the FDA.

This form of animal testing, called cosmetics and personal care product testing, was banned in the European Union in 2003. European Union companies cannot market personal care products that have been tested on animals. Israel banned animal testing on personal care products in 2007. Israel then banned imported products that used animal testing in 2013.

European laws have forced Americans to think about animal testing on cosmetics. The Humane Society of the United States and the Physicians Committee for

People for the Ethical Treatment of Animals (PETA) activists in India speak out against selling products that are tested on animals in 2014.

Responsible Medicine joined forces to try to pass a similar law in the United States. The Humane Cosmetics Act was introduced in the House of Representatives in 2014. Its goal is to end animal testing on cosmetics and hygiene products.

According to polling data published by the Humane Society, 73 percent of Americans polled support a ban on cosmetics testing. But that does not guarantee the success of the bill. Antivivisectionists hope that the Humane Cosmetics Act will become law and that it will be the first of many steps toward a ban on all animal testing.

WHAT DO YOU THINK?

- Do you think animal testing can ever be justified? If so, under what circumstances? If not, why?

- If you had a choice between buying toothpaste that has not been tested on animals and toothpaste that has been tested on animals, which one would you choose? What if the toothpaste that had not been tested on animals cost twice as much as the other toothpaste?

- Anyone who has had to take medicines, such as antibiotics or vaccines, has benefited from animal testing. Knowing this, do you think that you are also responsible for the animals in testing facilities? Or are only the scientists directly involved in testing responsible?

- The FDA requires all new medicines to be tested on animals before they can be tested on people. If you could rewrite the law, would it require animal testing or alternatives to animal testing?

TABLE OF CONTENTS

CHAPTER 1
THE GREATER GOOD

CHAPTER 2
ANIMAL TESTING HAS A PURPOSE

CHAPTER 3
SAVING HUMAN LIVES

CHAPTER 4
THE FUTURE OF ANIMAL TESTING

WHAT DO YOU THINK?

INDEX

Shared Resources

THE GREATER GOOD

High school senior Eric Pelly received a hard hit during a rugby match and was rushed to the hospital. Doctors diagnosed the Pennsylvania 18-year-old with a severe concussion, his fourth. They told him he could not play sports for the next three months. Eric was dead 10 days later. The concussion had caused swelling and bleeding in his brain, cutting off his oxygen supply. Eric's doctors reviewed information from his coaches and teammates. It described other hard hits Eric had experienced during games. Eric's death was nearly 10 years ago. Today scientists hope to prevent tragedies such as Eric Pelly's death by studying the effects of repetitive brain injuries on rats.

4

A Beacon of Hope

At Boston University teams of scientists study types of dementia, such as Alzheimer's, and Parkinson's disease, a disorder of the nervous system. They also study brain injuries, including those caused by sports accidents. Their work shows how damaging and dangerous repetitive brain injuries are. Brain tissue damage caused by repetitive brain injuries takes a long time to heal. Athletes who have experienced repeated concussions are four times more likely to develop Alzheimer's or Parkinson's disease. They typically develop these diseases at a younger age than

Studying brain injuries in rats has helped scientists learn more about repetitive brain injuries in athletes.

normal. In addition, they have a higher risk of seizures, depression, and violent aggression.

The symptoms of concussion are headache, nausea, dizziness, and confusion. If a patient doesn't have these symptoms, doctors do not diagnose a concussion. But as researchers at West Virginia University School of Medicine have recently learned, an absence of concussion symptoms does not rule out a brain injury.

The scientists replicated hard hits, such as the ones Eric Pelly experienced, on rats in their lab. Then they observed the rats' behavior for one week. They found no symptoms of concussion in the rats' behavior, even though the rats had received hard hits. The scientists euthanized the rats to study their brain tissue. The brain tissue showed damage caused by the hard hits. The tests on rats proved that brain injury can be present even if there are no symptoms of concussion.

Primates and Cognitive Science

Cognitive science is the study of how people think and remember. These abilities can be damaged by brain injuries or mental illness. Primate brains are the most similar to human brains. So scientists study monkeys to find ways to treat and cure humans. They look at how brain-damaged macaques tell the difference between various objects. They observe how reducing serotonin in the brain causes marmosets to behave in ways similar to humans with obsessive-compulsive disorder or schizophrenia. Scientists hope that this research will lead to better treatments for humans with brain injuries or mental illness.

Animal research on mice brain injuries has proven hard hits in sports are damaging to the brain even if there are no visible signs of injury.

A Brighter Future

The study of mice has also helped scientists learn more about memory loss. Scientists at the Salk Cellular Neurobiology Laboratory in southern California developed J147, a drug that improves memory in mice. J147 may not work on humans. But its potential to reverse memory loss in humans brings hope to people who suffer from dementia. It may also help people who have suffered brain injuries. Scientists hope to continue their tests on lab animals to find new and better treatments for those who have suffered brain injuries and memory loss.

ANIMAL TESTING HAS A PURPOSE

Animals have been used in scientific testing since at least the 500s BCE, when Greek philosopher and scientist Aristotle wrote about his experiments on animals. Five hundred years later, Roman physicians dissected animals to learn how their body systems worked. And during the 1100s, Arab physicians practiced surgeries on animals before trying them on humans. As scientists' understanding of the animal body improved, so did their ability to heal.

The 1800s and 1900s saw rapid changes in science and medicine. Diseases that were once deadly could now be prevented or cured. These changes were due

in large part to the experiments scientists conducted on animals.

Emil von Behring studied diphtheria in guinea pigs in the 1880s and 1890s. Diphtheria is an upper respiratory illness and skin disease caused by bacteria. Von Behring found a way to kill the bacteria. This led to the development of the diphtheria antitoxin for use in people. Frederick Banting studied dogs to isolate insulin in 1921. He used his research to treat diabetes in humans. Corwin Hinshaw and William

Dr. Albert Sabin holds a chimpanzee in a Cincinnati research laboratory during polio vaccination testing in 1956.

Feldman experimented on guinea pigs to find a cure for tuberculosis in the 1930s and 1940s. And in the 1940s and 1950s, Jonas Salk and Albert Sabin experimented on rhesus monkeys and chimpanzees to develop polio vaccines. The polio vaccines were powerful. In the first three years of their use, new polio cases in the United States decreased by more than 85 percent.

What Is Animal Testing?

Animals are used in research because they are full biological systems. That means they are living, breathing organisms. Much like humans, they have neurological (brain and nerves), cardiopulmonary (heart and lungs), and digestive (stomach and intestines) systems that work together to keep them alive.

Scientists experiment on animals when they want to see how a full biological system will react to a new chemical or drug. They also experiment on animals when they want to see how a full biological system will react to an event, such as a hard hit. And they experiment on animals when they want to use a full biological system to practice new surgical procedures. Animal experiments can be done on living or dead animals. When scientists test chemicals, drugs, or behavior on living animals, it is called vivisection.

It's the Law

Before new medications can be sold in the United States, they must pass a series of tests. The tests prove they are safe for people. The U.S. Food and Drug Administration (FDA) oversees the tests. The FDA says that human tests cannot be done if the test involves giving a healthy human a "potentially lethal or permanently disabling … substance." In such cases the FDA says new drugs, vaccines, and products should first be tested on animals.

Dissection

Students often participate in a type of animal testing called dissection. Students are given the body of a dead animal, such as a frog or a fetal pig. They cut the animal apart and observe its body systems and organs. Biology teachers use dissection as a tool to teach students about anatomy. Susan Offner, writing in the *American Biology Teacher* journal, explains why teachers believe dissection is an important part of students' education: "No model, no video, no diagram and no movie can duplicate the fascination, the sense of discovery, wonder and even awe that students feel when they find real structures in their own specimens."

If the animal tests show that the new drug, vaccine, or product works on animals the way the scientists hope it will work on humans, then it can move on to the next step. Eventually all new drugs, vaccines, and products will be tested on thousands of humans before they can be sold.

Barriers to Animal Testing

Band of Mercy, an organization opposed to animal testing, burned a lab being built by Hoechst Pharmaceuticals in 1973 in England. Since then scientists who use animals in research have been criticized. Animal rights activists

increased public campaigns against scientists. They protested in front of scientists' labs. They even picketed in front of their houses. Activists also filed lawsuits in an attempt to shut labs down. In the most extreme cases, activists broke into labs and destroyed equipment.

Animal rights activists gathered to protest the proposed building of a new lab at England's University of Oxford. Sixteen-year-old Laurie Pycroft saw the protesters in the news. He also decided to protest in 2006. But he had a different agenda. He showed up at the site of the protest with a couple of friends and a sign that read, "Support Progress—Build the Oxford Lab!" Pycroft decided to found Pro-Test, an organization dedicated to educating the public about the importance of animal testing.

Seeing a young student stand up to the animal rights activists encouraged scientists to join Pycroft. Four weeks later Pro-Test led a rally in support of animal experimentation for scientific research. More than 700 people joined. Inspired by Pro-Test rallies, Italian scientists and students in Milan demonstrated in 2013 to raise awareness for the need for animals in lab tests. Supporters of animal experimentation hope communication and openness will help scientists and animal rights groups find common ground.

Pro-Test founder Laurie Pycroft (right) defends animal testing outside the University of Oxford in 2006.

A World without Animal Testing

Scientists such as those involved with Pro-Test believe animal testing improves the quality of human life. During the animal testing phase of a research project, scientists look to answer questions. How does this chemical affect skin? How does it affect organs, such as the liver, heart, or stomach? How does it affect behavior? To find out, scientists may rub the product on an animal's skin or eyes. They may inject the animal with it. Then they observe. Scientists report their results to the FDA. This is an expensive process. But it serves an important purpose. When drugs, vaccines, or products are first tested on

Pro-Test members march outside of the University of California, Los Angeles, in 2009.

animals, animal testing proponents argue that scientists are better able to keep humans safe.

More than 100 people died when they ingested elixir sulfanilamide in 1937. Sulfanilamide was a popular treatment for sore throats in the 1930s. But it was given in tablet form. Not all patients could take tablets easily, so chemist Harold Cole Watkins at S. E. Massengill Company in Tennessee created elixir sulfanilamide. It was a liquid medicine instead of a tablet. What Watkins did not know was that the chemical he used to dissolve the sulfanilamide, diethylene glycol, was poisonous. He hadn't tested it on animals before selling it.

In hopes of preventing future disasters, the FDA passed the Federal Food, Drug, and Cosmetic Act in 1938. It has been added to and changed as scientists continue to test and learn. For example, in 1962 the FDA said drugs that are approved for one treatment cannot be used for another treatment. The consequences of not testing a drug on animals came to light in the 1950s and 1960s. During those years, doctors prescribed thalidomide to people to treat colds, headaches, and nausea during pregnancy. More than 10,000 children whose pregnant mothers took it for nausea were born with birth defects, including missing arms and legs. Thalidomide had not been tested on pregnant animals first. Today the FDA sets higher standards

The Federal Food, Drug, and Cosmetic Act stated there must be adequate labeling on all drugs for safe use.

for drug testing. Before a drug can even make it to the animal testing stage, it must first pass metabolic studies that prove the drug will be safe in human tissue. These new regulations are designed to save human lives and prevent unintended side effects.

SAVING HUMAN LIVES

Mice and rats make good subjects for animal testing because they share many organ functions with humans. Chimpanzees are even more closely related. Chimps and humans share more than 98 percent of their DNA. Humans and mice share more than 95 percent of their DNA.

Genes, which are made up of DNA, are parts of cells that influence a living thing's appearance and growth. Genes determine physical characteristics, such as height and hair color. Genes also point to diseases that are passed from one generation to the next.

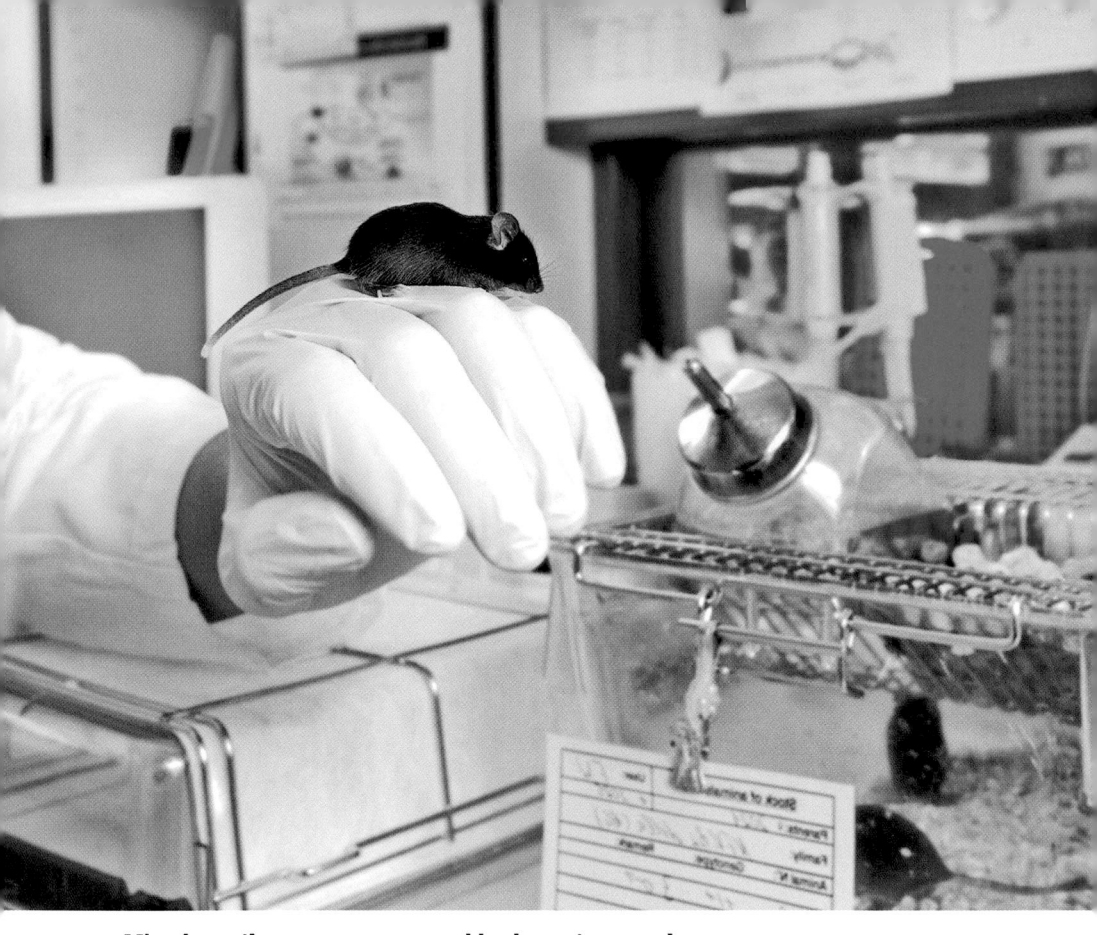

Mice have the same organs and body systems as humans.

The Animal Model

Because of their genetic similarity, chimpanzees and other apes have been used in experiments. Albert Sabin used them in his experiments to find a vaccine for polio. Scientists have also used chimps to study forms of hepatitis, a disease that attacks the liver.

Dogs and cats are also used in labs. More than 72,000 dogs and 24,000 cats were experimented on in science labs in the United States in 2012. Dogs and cats are often used when a new drug for animals, such as heartworm

Animal testing is beneficial for animals too, creating disease-fighting medicines for dogs.

medicine, is created. Veterinarians also try out new surgical procedures on cats and dogs.

Of all animals experimented on in science labs in the United States, most are mice, rats, birds, and fish. There are no definite numbers of mice, rats, and birds used in labs because the Animal Welfare Act does not always

Saving Babies

Every year 40,000 babies are born in the United States with heart defects. Many of the children need new hearts. Worldwide, approximately 350 children receive heart transplants each year. Heart transplants give the children longer lives and a better quality of life. Before hearts were transplanted in humans, scientists practiced organ transplants on animals. Alexis Carrel won a Nobel Prize in 1912 for his research in organ transplants with dogs and cats.

cover them. Scientists estimate that from 13 million to 25 million mice and rats are used in labs in the United States each year. Since rats and mice are much smaller than chimpanzees, dogs, and cats, they are easier and less expensive to house and confine. They also have shorter life cycles and reproduce quickly, so there is a constant supply of them. And scientists have learned how to breed mice so that they can copy human diseases. Scientists do this by changing the genes of the mice they breed. This allows them to learn new ways to treat diseases.

Whose Life Is More Important?

So how do scientists decide to test on animals? They consider how a new vaccine or drug could improve the

lives of humans. Polio is a terrifying disease. It was even more frightening before a vaccine to prevent it became available in 1955. Those affected by the virus experienced crippling in their arms and legs and even paralysis of the muscles in their respiratory systems. Polio affected children more than adults, and even today, there is no cure.

Polio researchers had tested their vaccines on more than 9,000 monkeys and 150 chimpanzees. Scientists decided that the human lives saved by the polio vaccines were more important than the animals that died to make the vaccines possible. And the American public agreed. Households across the United States sent their pennies, nickels, and dimes to the March of Dimes Foundation to fund research for a polio vaccine.

Other Options

There are other options for testing that do not involve euthanizing animal subjects. One involves in vitro experiments—tests on tissues in test tubes. In this process scientists collect cells from an animal. The animal they collect the tissue from does not have to be killed. Scientists use special tools to scrape off the animal tissue they need to observe. This allows scientists to observe how chemicals react with tissue.

In vitro testing is successful in killing viruses in a test tube, but it does not always translate to a full biological system.

Scientists test tissue samples as a step in the process of developing new vaccines and drugs. If tissue reacts badly to the chemicals, the experiment does not go any further. For example, there are many chemicals, including bleach and chlorine, that kill viruses and bacteria in a test tube. But they can't be used to kill those same viruses and bacteria in a living animal because they are poisonous. If the tissue reacts to the chemicals the way scientists hope it will, then they will test it on a living animal.

THE FUTURE OF ANIMAL TESTING

There is no doubt animal testing has helped develop cures for human disease. But the way people view animal testing has changed. Most Americans supported scientific research, including animal testing, in the mid-1900s. They saw how it resulted in new vaccines and medications. They also saw how the diphtheria antitoxin cured people who would have died and how the polio vaccine prevented the spread of polio.

Journalists working undercover documented the inhumane living conditions of animals in research facilities, publishing articles in national magazines such as *Sports Illustrated* and *LIFE* beginning in the

Many Americans saw the positive effects of animal testing in the form of the polio vaccine in the 1950s.

mid-1960s. And by the 1980s lawsuits were brought against laboratories for inhumane treatment of animals. The tide was shifting. No longer did the American public wholeheartedly support the scientists and researchers who conducted tests on animals.

Animal rights activists began public campaigns and protests against scientists. Public outcry did not stop animal testing. It did, however, make scientists' work more difficult. Despite the protests, scientists continued experimenting on animals, testing cosmetics, hygiene products, new vaccines, and medications. But without public support, scientists had a harder time finding the funds to pay for their important research.

The Basel Declaration of 2010

With the founding of Pro-Test and similar organizations, scientists realized they needed to find a new way to change people's minds about animal testing. Keeping their work secret did not help. So they decided to encourage people to talk about animal testing in a polite, civil way.

Scientists around the world signed an agreement called the Basel Declaration in 2010. The declaration said that animal testing was important and must continue. It also stated that experiments on animals must protect animal welfare by following the 3Rs of animal testing.

The goal of the 3Rs is to make sure animal testing is done only when it is necessary and only to improve human or animal lives. The first R stands for replacement. Scientists should use a nonanimal model whenever they can. The second R stands for reduction. Scientists should use fewer animals whenever they can. The third R stands

Public outcry against animal testing continues. Animal rights activists demonstrate against animal testing in Paris in 2014.

for refinement. Scientists should always try to improve the living conditions of lab animals and reduce stress and pain whenever they can. Scientists in many countries, including Canada, the United Kingdom, the European Union, and the United States, have committed to the 3Rs of animal testing.

Animal Testing Must Continue

The scientists who signed the Basel Declaration believe animal testing must continue. One of their arguments involves the treatment of infectious diseases. These diseases, which can pass from person to person, have

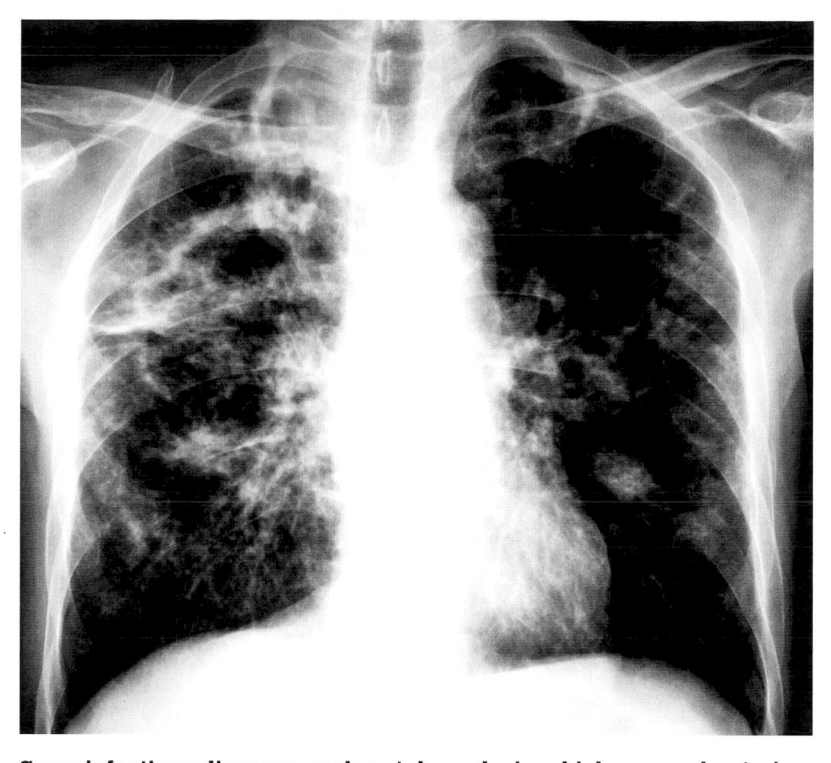

Some infectious diseases, such as tuberculosis, which causes bacteria to grow in the lungs, require animal testing to find new medications.

changed over time. Many of them cannot always be cured with medications that are available today. Scientists must find new medications to treat these old diseases. When they discover new ways to combine chemicals, they need to test them to see if they work. Even if scientists know how a living body reacts to each of the chemicals in the new combination, they don't know how a living body will react to the combination itself. It is easier and safer to test these new combinations on animals than on people.

It is also important to consider the law when it comes to animal experiments. If new drugs and vaccines are not tested on animals before they are given to people, people

become the subjects of the experiment. The law is clear on this: new drugs and vaccines must show that they are safe and effective before they can be given to humans. One way to show they are safe is to test them on animals. Even if the law were to change, finding enough people to agree to test new drugs or vaccines would be difficult. If humans participate in experiments, they must consent to it. Not many people would agree to consume chemicals that may not be safe.

The financial cost of using only humans in lab tests is greater than the cost of using animals. In addition, humans consent to the tests and are paid. And should anything go wrong with the tests, humans are paid even more money, making human-only lab tests more expensive than animal lab tests.

Research Saves Animal Lives Too

Animals suffer from many of the same illnesses as people. They develop asthma, cancer, diabetes, and infections. Animals can even have kidney disease or go blind. And because of genetic similarities between humans and other mammals, many of the same drugs and vaccines can treat and prevent illness and disease in both humans and animals.

Many treatments and medications that were meant to help people are now used to help animals. Dogs diagnosed with diabetes can receive insulin treatments, just like people. Cats diagnosed with asthma can receive the medication they need, just like people. And pets that need blood transfusions can be saved, just like people.

Where Research Is Headed

Traumatic brain injuries, Alzheimer's, multiple sclerosis, and spinal cord injuries are all focal points for research scientists today, and with good reason. More than 5.4 million Americans are living with Alzheimer's. More than 400,000 people are living with multiple sclerosis, which breaks down cells in the brain and spinal cord.

With animal testing, scientists have made hopeful steps toward developing drugs that will prevent or reverse memory loss from Alzheimer's or brain injury and improve safety for athletes. But there is more work to be done. Until scientists have discovered cures for cancer and viruses such as HIV, animal testing will continue to be a necessary part of their research.

WHAT DO YOU THINK?

- Do you think vivisection is acceptable? Why or why not?

- Do you think there are some forms of vivisection that are more acceptable than others? If so, what makes one type of vivisection better than another?

- If you were a scientist who conducted experiments on animals, would you want to have open conversations about your work? Or would you prefer to do your work in private?

- What do you think would be a fair system of regulating the care of animals in testing facilities?

INDEX

GLOSSARY

antivivisection—against experimenting on living animals for science

dementia—a brain condition in which the ability to think or remember deteriorates

dissection—the act of cutting a plant or animal into separate parts for examination and study

DNA—an acid located in the nucleus of a cell that is the chemical basis for heredity

Draize test—a test performed on animals, often for testing cosmetics, which involves dripping or rubbing a substance on the animal's eyes or skin to observe its effects

euthanize—the act of killing a sick or injured animal with as little pain as possible

genetic—relating to the part of DNA that contains information needed to control inherited traits

vivisection—operating or experimenting on a living animal for scientific or medical study

welfare—the state of doing well, especially in relation to happiness or well-being

INTERNET SITES

Use FactHound to find Internet sites related to this book. All of the sites on FactHound have been researched by our staff.

Here's all you do:
Visit *www.facthound.com*
Type in this code: 9780756549961

1

PROS AND CONS: LIFESAVING RESEARCH

Pros

Animal testing has led to cures and treatments of human diseases, including diabetes, polio, and tuberculosis.

There is no comparable alternative to the living animal system.

Animals make good models for the human body because of genetic similarities.

In some cases it would be unethical to test on people, so animal tests must be used instead.

Cons

There are alternatives to animal testing that can and should be used instead.

Animals and humans are genetically similar, but they are not the same.

Products can pass safety testing in animals and still not be safe for humans.

Animal testing is inhumane.

PROS AND CONS: ANIMAL WELFARE

Pros

The Animal Welfare Act requires researchers to use nonanimal experiments whenever possible.

The USDA requires research labs to provide safe shelter, food, and water for all animals being tested.

The 3Rs of animal testing—replacement, reduction, and refinement—have helped improve the conditions of animal testing.

Cons

The Animal Welfare Act does not protect or monitor 95 percent of the animals being tested in the United States.

Although the USDA requires research labs to provide shelter, the shelter may only be a small cage.

Approximately 25 million animals live in U.S. research labs.

CRITICAL THINKING USING THE COMMON CORE

1. Consider both perspectives in this book. Do you believe that animal testing is necessary? Do you think animal testing is too cruel? Create an outline for a paragraph that explains your opinion. Include a topic sentence. In the body of your paragraph, use at least three quotes from the text to support your opinion. (Key Ideas and Details)

2. On page 11 of Lifesaving Research, Susan Offner explains why dissection, a form of animal experimentation, should continue. She believes dissection is important and necessary to learn about animals. Do you think dissection is necessary, or do you think other methods, such as videos and diagrams, are sufficient for learning about animals? Write a paragraph, describing your opinion. How would you persuade others to think as you do? Support your ideas with two or three credible sources found online or in books. (Integration of Knowledge and Ideas)

3. Pick one side of the argument to create a cluster diagram. In the center bubble, write the main idea of the argument. Then add at least three other bubbles with examples from the text of points that support that side. When you're done, explain why these examples support the side of the argument to a classmate or your teacher. (Integration of Knowledge and Ideas)

BOOKS IN THIS SERIES

Animal Testing: Lifesaving Research vs. Animal Welfare

Punishing Bullies: Zero Tolerance vs. Working Together

School Lunches: Healthy Choices vs. Crowd Pleasers

Social Media: Like It or Leave It

SELECT BIBLIOGRAPHY

"Animals Used in Research." National Anti-Vivisection Society. 7 May 2014. http://www.navs.org/science/animals-used-in-research

"Animal Welfare Act Violations at Ivy League Universities." Physicians Committee for Responsible Medicine. September 2011. 7 May 2014. http://www.pcrm.org/research/edtraining/ivy-league/awa-violations-at-ivy-league-detailed-results

"Biomedical Research." The Humane Society of the United States. May 2014. 9 May 2014. http://www.humanesociety.org/issues/biomedical_research/#.U2qzU8cteMI

Franco, Nuno Henrique. "Animal Experiments in Biomedical Research: A Historical Perspective." National Anti-Vivisection Society. 19 March 2013. 26 April 2014. http://www.navs.org/science/history-of-vivisection

"Scientific and Humane Issues in the Use of Random Source Dogs and Cats in Research." National Center for Biotechnology Information. 2009. 7 May 2014. http://www.ncbi.nlm.nih.gov/books/NBK32669/

"The Shot Heard 'Round the World: Development of the Salk Polio Vaccine." University of Pittsburgh School of Pharmacy. 27 April 2014. http://museum.pharmacy.pitt.edu/salk/

FURTHER READING

Coster, Patience. *The Debate about Animal Testing.* New York: Rosen Publishing, 2011.

Hunnicutt, Susan. *Animal Experimentation.* Farmington Hills, Mich.: Greenhaven Press/Gale Cengage Learning, 2013.

Mack, Gail. *Animal Rights.* New York: Marshall Cavendish Benchmark, 2012.

Watson, Stephanie. *Animal Testing: Issues and Ethics.* New York: Rosen Pub. Group, 2009.